To add, join numbers of things together. Use the **+** sign.
Then count how many things there are in all.

| 2 birds | + | 3 birds | = | 5 birds in all |

Write a number sentence for each picture story.

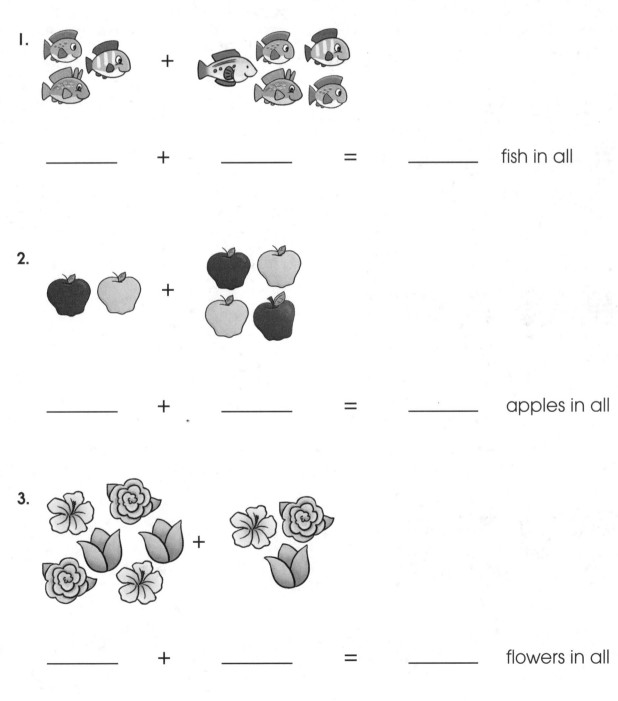

1.

_____ + _____ = _____ fish in all

2.

_____ + _____ = _____ apples in all

3.

_____ + _____ = _____ flowers in all

Subtraction Number Sentences

To subtract, start with a number of things. Take some away. Use the **–** sign.
Then count the number of the things that are left.

5 mice in all

5 mice – 2 mice = 3 mice left

Write a number sentence for each picture story.

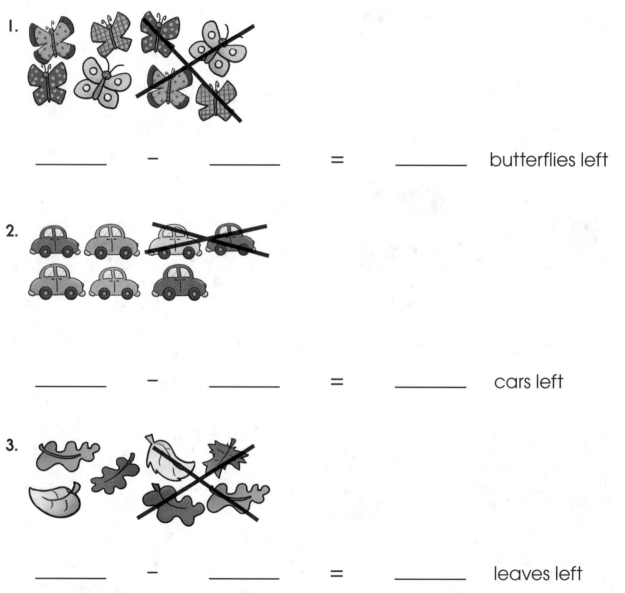

1. _____ – _____ = _____ butterflies left

2. _____ – _____ = _____ cars left

3. _____ – _____ = _____ leaves left

Read the problem. Then add or subtract to find the answer.

Sue had 4 socks.
She bought 2 more socks.
How many socks does she have in all?

Solve

$$\begin{array}{r} 4 \\ +2 \\ \hline 6 \end{array}$$ socks

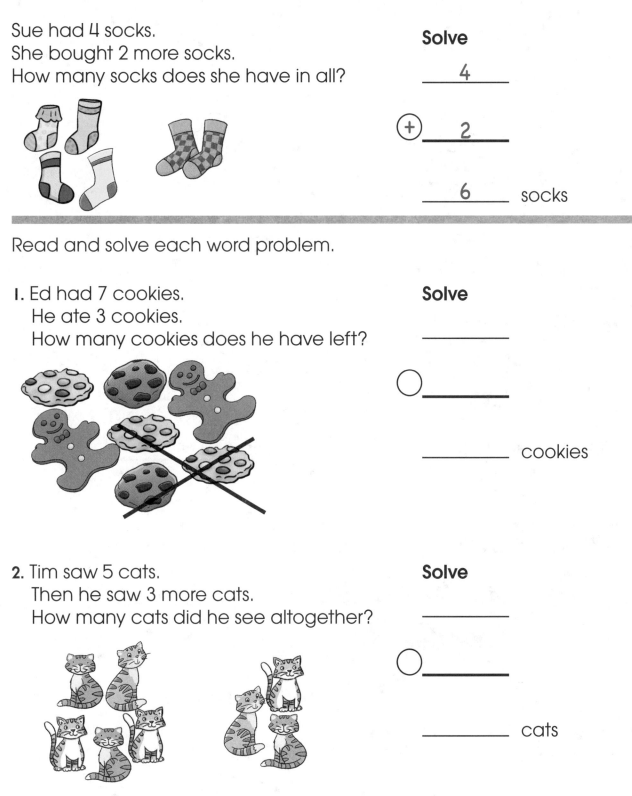

Read and solve each word problem.

1. Ed had 7 cookies.
   He ate 3 cookies.
   How many cookies does he have left?

Solve

_____ cookies

2. Tim saw 5 cats.
   Then he saw 3 more cats.
   How many cats did he see altogether?

Solve

_____ cats

More Word Problems to Solve

Read the problem. Then add or subtract to find the answer.

Luis had 10 pieces of candy.
He ate 4 of them.
How many pieces of candy are left?

Solve

$$\begin{array}{r} 10 \\ -\ \underline{4} \\ 6 \end{array}$$ pieces of candy

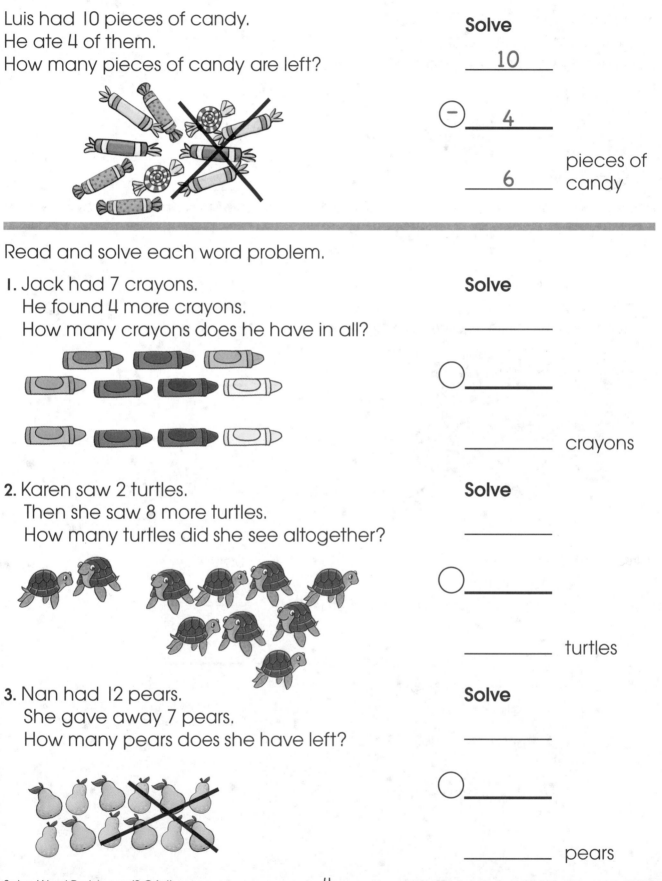

Read and solve each word problem.

1. Jack had 7 crayons.
   He found 4 more crayons.
   How many crayons does he have in all?

   Solve

   _____
   ◯ _____

   _____ crayons

2. Karen saw 2 turtles.
   Then she saw 8 more turtles.
   How many turtles did she see altogether?

   Solve

   _____
   ◯ _____

   _____ turtles

3. Nan had 12 pears.
   She gave away 7 pears.
   How many pears does she have left?

   Solve

   _____
   ◯ _____

   _____ pears

Finding Sums

The answer to an addition problem is called the **sum**.

$3 + 4 = \underline{7}$

Look at the pictures. Read the number sentence.
Write the sum.

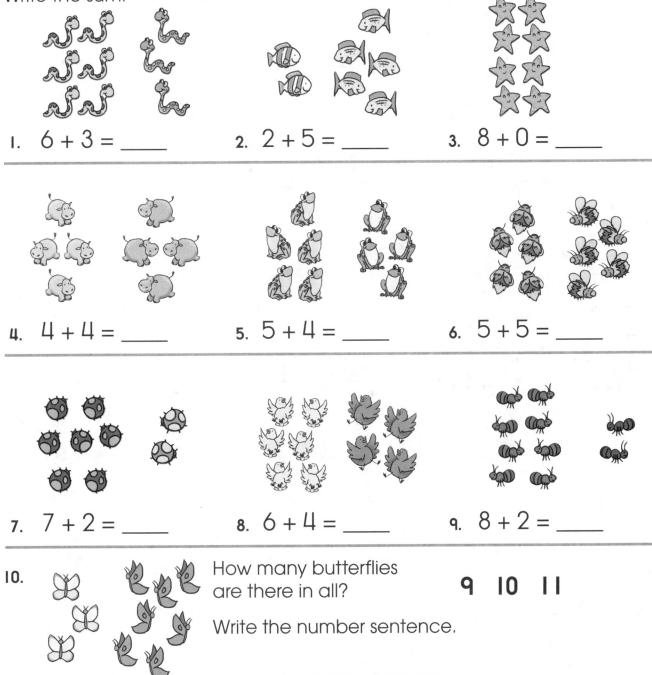

1. $6 + 3 = \underline{}$

2. $2 + 5 = \underline{}$

3. $8 + 0 = \underline{}$

4. $4 + 4 = \underline{}$

5. $5 + 4 = \underline{}$

6. $5 + 5 = \underline{}$

7. $7 + 2 = \underline{}$

8. $6 + 4 = \underline{}$

9. $8 + 2 = \underline{}$

10. How many butterflies are there in all?   **9   10   11**

Write the number sentence.

_____

Finding Sums (2.OA.2)

Fact Families

A **fact family** uses the same numbers in it's addition and subtraction problems.

8, 7, 15

$$\underline{8} + \underline{7} = \underline{15}$$
$$\underline{7} + \underline{8} = \underline{15}$$
$$\underline{15} - \underline{7} = \underline{8}$$
$$\underline{15} - \underline{8} = \underline{7}$$

Complete the fact family.

1. 5, 9, 14

$$\underline{5} + \underline{\quad} = \underline{\quad}$$
$$\underline{9} + \underline{\quad} = \underline{\quad}$$
$$\underline{14} - \underline{\quad} = \underline{\quad}$$
$$\underline{\quad} - \underline{\quad} = \underline{5}$$

2. 9, 6, 15

$$\underline{\quad} + \underline{\quad} = \underline{\quad}$$
$$\underline{\quad} + \underline{\quad} = \underline{\quad}$$
$$\underline{\quad} - \underline{\quad} = \underline{\quad}$$
$$\underline{\quad} - \underline{\quad} = \underline{\quad}$$

3. 7, 6, 13

$$\underline{\quad} + \underline{\quad} = \underline{\quad}$$
$$\underline{\quad} + \underline{\quad} = \underline{\quad}$$
$$\underline{\quad} - \underline{\quad} = \underline{\quad}$$
$$\underline{\quad} - \underline{\quad} = \underline{\quad}$$

4. 8, 9, 17

$$\underline{\quad} + \underline{\quad} = \underline{\quad}$$
$$\underline{\quad} + \underline{\quad} = \underline{\quad}$$
$$\underline{\quad} - \underline{\quad} = \underline{\quad}$$
$$\underline{\quad} - \underline{\quad} = \underline{\quad}$$

5. 8, 6, 14

$$\underline{\quad} + \underline{\quad} = \underline{\quad}$$
$$\underline{\quad} + \underline{\quad} = \underline{\quad}$$
$$\underline{\quad} - \underline{\quad} = \underline{\quad}$$
$$\underline{\quad} - \underline{\quad} = \underline{\quad}$$

6. 7, 9, 16

$$\underline{\quad} + \underline{\quad} = \underline{\quad}$$
$$\underline{\quad} + \underline{\quad} = \underline{\quad}$$
$$\underline{\quad} - \underline{\quad} = \underline{\quad}$$
$$\underline{\quad} - \underline{\quad} = \underline{\quad}$$

$$\begin{array}{cccc} 8 & 4 & 12 & 12 \\ +4 & +8 & -4 & -8 \\ \hline 12 & 12 & 8 & 4 \end{array}$$

Write the missing numbers to complete the fact family.

1.
$$\begin{array}{cccc} 5 & 7 & 12 & 12 \\ +7 & +5 & -5 & -7 \\ \hline \square & \square & \square & \square \end{array}$$

2.
$$\begin{array}{cc} 5 & 10 \\ +\square & -5 \\ \hline 10 & \square \end{array}$$

3.
$$\begin{array}{cccc} 3 & 6 & 9 & 9 \\ +\square & +3 & -\square & -3 \\ \hline 9 & \square & 3 & \square \end{array}$$

4.
$$\begin{array}{cc} 6 & \square \\ +6 & -6 \\ \hline \square & 6 \end{array}$$

5.
$$\begin{array}{cccc} 6 & \square & 11 & 11 \\ +5 & +6 & -\square & -6 \\ \hline \square & 11 & 6 & \square \end{array}$$

6.
$$\begin{array}{cccc} 7 & 4 & 11 & \square \\ +\square & +7 & -7 & -4 \\ \hline 11 & \square & \square & 7 \end{array}$$

Which Number Is Missing?

Find the missing numbers.

1.
$$6 + \boxed{} = 10$$
$$10 - 6 = \boxed{}$$

2.
$$14 - 8 = \boxed{}$$
$$\boxed{} + 8 = 14$$

3.
$$3 + \boxed{} = 12$$
$$12 - \boxed{} = 9$$

4.
$$7 + \boxed{} = 13$$
$$13 - \boxed{} = 6$$

5.
$$15 - 8 = \boxed{}$$
$$\boxed{} + 7 = 15$$

6.
$$9 + \boxed{} = 18$$
$$18 - \boxed{} = 9$$

7. $4 + \boxed{} = 11$

$11 - 4 = \boxed{}$

8. $7 + \boxed{} = 14$

$14 - \boxed{} = 7$

9. $6 + \boxed{} = 15$

$15 - 9 = \boxed{}$

10. $6 + \boxed{} = 12$

$12 - \boxed{} = 6$

11. $8 + \boxed{} = 17$

$17 - \boxed{} = 9$

12. $13 - 8 = \boxed{}$

$5 + \boxed{} = 13$

Sums and Differences

Solve this riddle:

Which animal would you hire to work in an office?

Add and subtract to find the answer.

A
6 + 7 = ____

E
3 + 9 = ____

T
14 – 7 = ____

S
16 – 8 = ____

A
5 + 8 = ____

R
18 – 9 = ____

E
4 + 8 = ____

R
17 – 8 = ____

R
15 – 6 = ____

S
15 – 7 = ____

Y
8 + 6 = ____

C
9 + 6 = ____

D
7 + 9 = ____

B
9 + 8 = ____

I
14 – 9 = ____

The ___ ___ ___ ___ ___ ___ ___ ___ ___
   8   12   15   9   12   7   13   9   14

___ ___ ___ ___
17 5 9 16

Add and Subtract within 20 (2.OA.2)

Checking Facts

Cross out the incorrect answers.
Which set has more correct answers? _____
Correct the incorrect answers in both sets.

Set A

$$\begin{array}{r} 7 \\ + 8 \\ \hline 15 \end{array} \qquad \begin{array}{r} 7 \\ + 5 \\ \hline 12 \end{array}$$

$$\begin{array}{r} 12 \\ - 6 \\ \hline 6 \end{array} \qquad \begin{array}{r} 15 \\ - 6 \\ \hline 8 \end{array}$$

$$\begin{array}{r} 9 \\ + 6 \\ \hline 14 \end{array} \qquad \begin{array}{r} 9 \\ + 4 \\ \hline 13 \end{array}$$

$$\begin{array}{r} 18 \\ - 9 \\ \hline 9 \end{array} \qquad \begin{array}{r} 17 \\ - 8 \\ \hline 8 \end{array}$$

Set B

$$\begin{array}{r} 5 \\ + 8 \\ \hline 13 \end{array} \qquad \begin{array}{r} 9 \\ + 7 \\ \hline 14 \end{array}$$

$$\begin{array}{r} 14 \\ - 7 \\ \hline 6 \end{array} \qquad \begin{array}{r} 15 \\ - 7 \\ \hline 8 \end{array}$$

$$\begin{array}{r} 4 \\ + 8 \\ \hline 12 \end{array} \qquad \begin{array}{r} 8 \\ + 6 \\ \hline 13 \end{array}$$

$$\begin{array}{r} 17 \\ - 9 \\ \hline 7 \end{array} \qquad \begin{array}{r} 15 \\ - 6 \\ \hline 9 \end{array}$$

Add and Subtract within 20 (2.OA.2)   © School Zone Publishing Company 02202

Even and Odd

An **even number** can be divided into groups of twos.
Six is an even number.

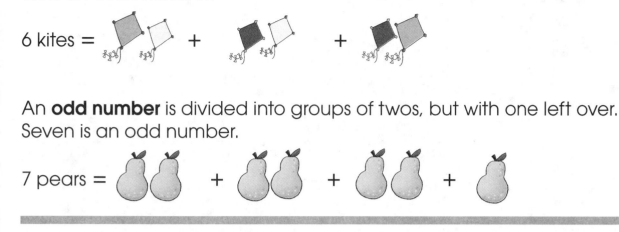

6 kites =

An **odd number** is divided into groups of twos, but with one left over.
Seven is an odd number.

7 pears =

Write number sentences for each number below using only **2**s and **1**s.
Then write either **even** or **odd** to describe the number.

1. 9 = _____ + _____ + _____ + _____ + _____   _____

2. 8 = _____ + _____ + _____ + _____   _____

3. 10 = _____ + _____ + _____ + _____ + _____   _____

4. Write all of the even numbers from 1–20.

_____

_____

5. Write all of the odd numbers from 1–20.

_____

_____

Counting by Twos, Fives, and Tens

Connect the dots.
Start at the ▲ and count by 2s to 50.
Start at the ● and count by 5s to 100.
Start at the ■ and count by 10s to 100.

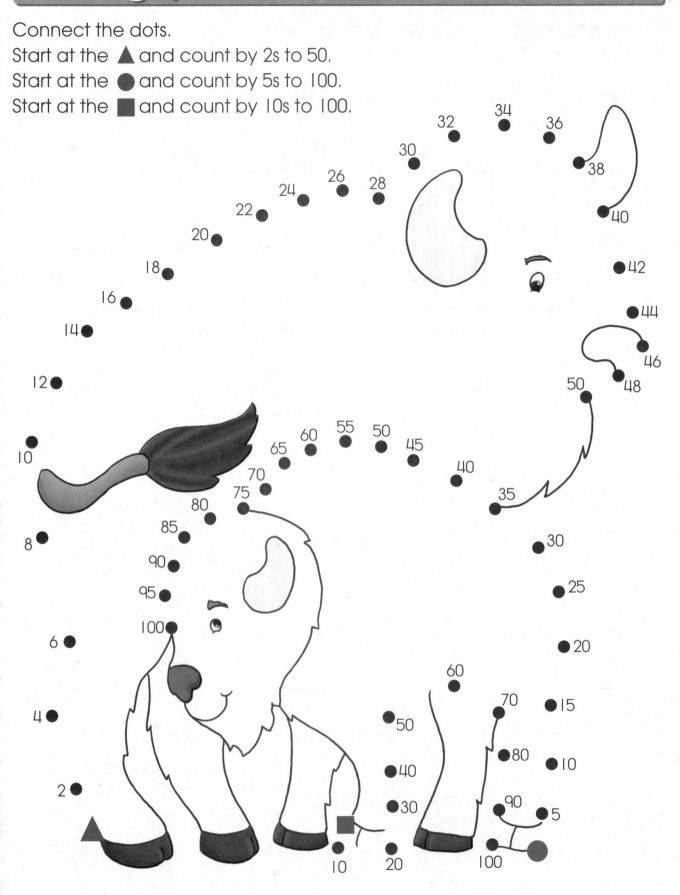

Adding Arrays

Write a number sentence for each array.
How many strawberries in each row? How many in all?

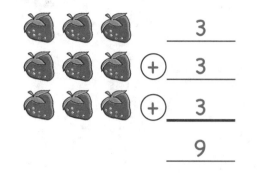

$$\underline{\hspace{1cm} 3 \hspace{1cm}}$$
$$+ \underline{\hspace{1cm} 3 \hspace{1cm}}$$
$$+ \underline{\hspace{1cm} 3 \hspace{1cm}}$$
$$\underline{\hspace{1cm} 9 \hspace{1cm}}$$

Write a number sentence for each array.

1.

○ _____
○ _____

_____

2.

_____
○ _____
○ _____
○ _____

_____

3.

_____
○ _____
○ _____
○ _____

_____

4.

_____
○ _____
○ _____

_____

5.

_____
○ _____

_____

6.

_____
○ _____
○ _____

_____

Adding Arrays (2.OA.4)

Write a number sentence for each array.
How many ducks in each row? How many in all?

$$
\begin{array}{r}
4 \\
+ \ 4 \\
+ \ 4 \\
\hline
12
\end{array}
$$

Write a number sentence for each array.

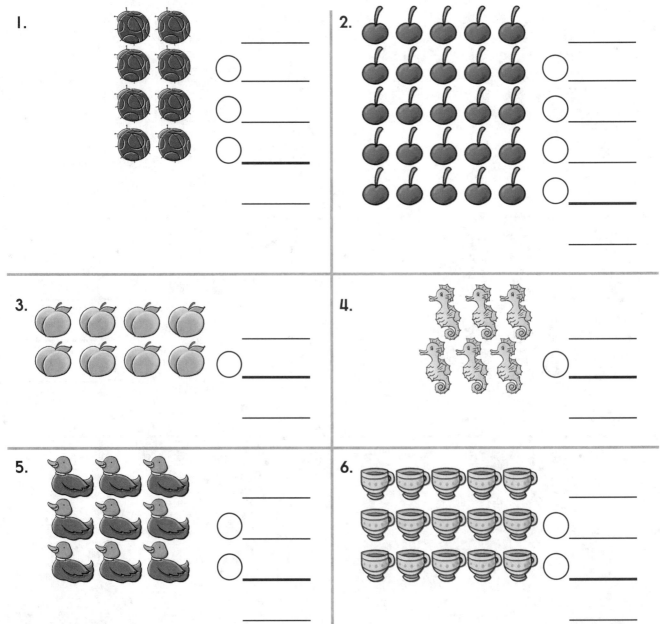

1.

2.

3.

4.

5.

6.

Tens and Ones

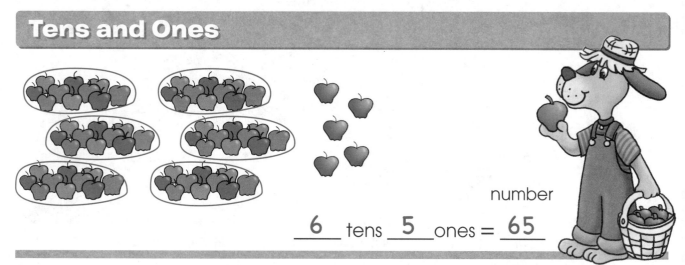

number

___6___ tens ___5___ ones = ___65___

Circle the groups of ten. Write the number of tens and ones.
Then write the number.

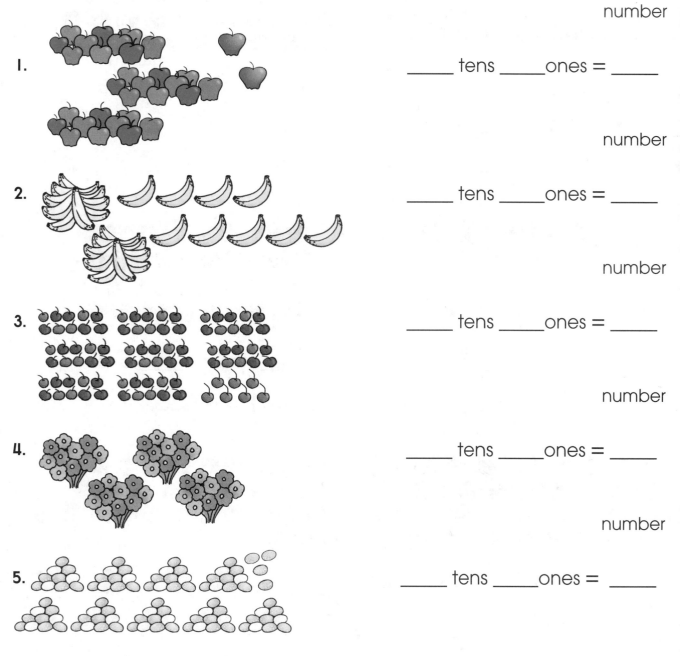

1.   number

____ tens ____ ones = ____

2.   number

____ tens ____ ones = ____

3.   number

____ tens ____ ones = ____

4.   number

____ tens ____ ones = ____

5.   number

____ tens ____ ones = ____

More about Tens and Ones

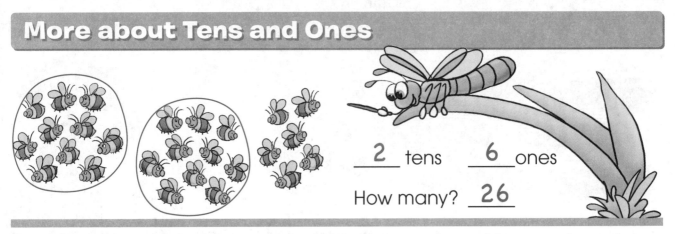

___2___ tens   ___6___ ones

How many? ___26___

Circle the objects in groups of ten. Write the number of tens and ones. Then write how many there are in all.

1.

_____ tens   _____ ones

How many? _____

2.

_____ tens   _____ ones

How many? _____

3.

_____ ten   _____ ones

How many? _____

4.

_____ tens   _____ ones

How many? _____

5.

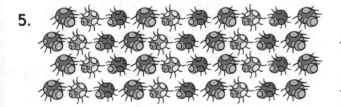 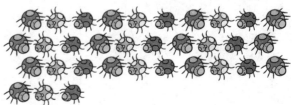

_____ tens   _____ ones

How many? _____

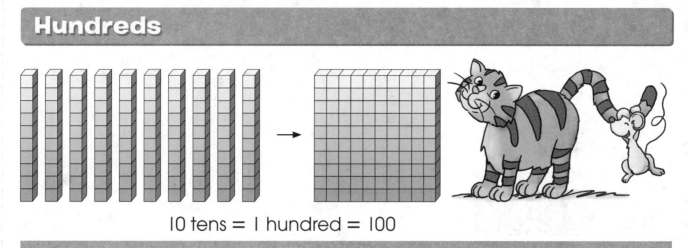

10 tens = 1 hundred = 100

Write how many hundreds there are. Then write the number.

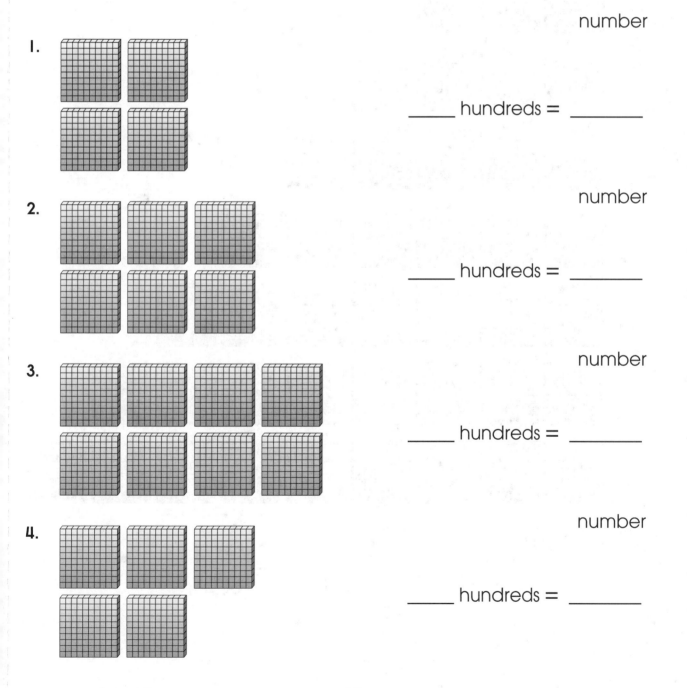

number

1.

_____ hundreds = _____

number

2.

_____ hundreds = _____

number

3.

_____ hundreds = _____

number

4.

_____ hundreds = _____

Write the number.

Connect the dots.
Count by 100s to 900.

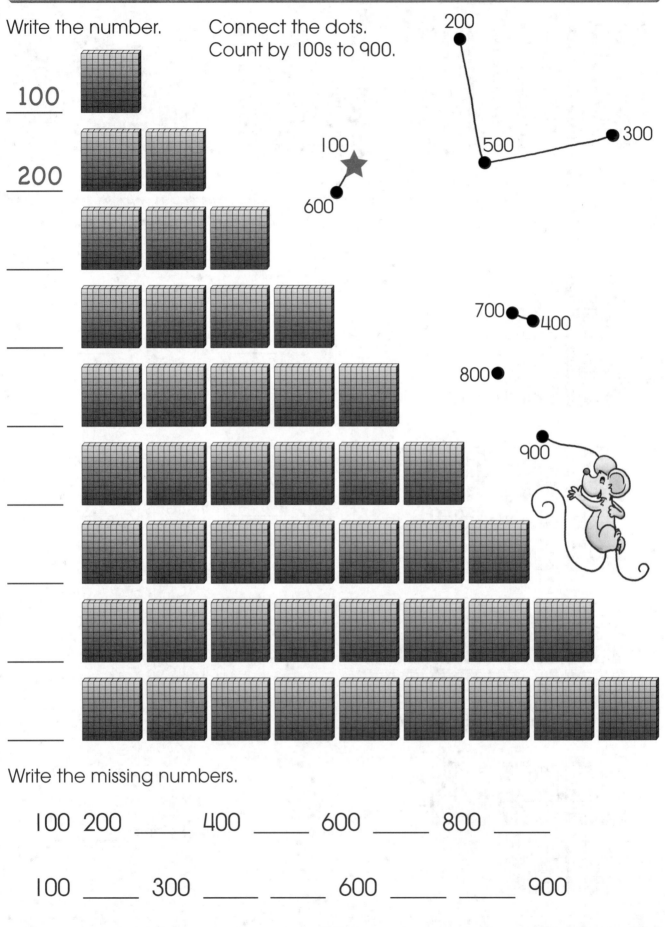

100

200

_____

_____

_____

_____

_____

_____

_____

Write the missing numbers.

100 200 _____ 400 _____ 600 _____ 800 _____

100 _____ 300 _____ _____ 600 _____ _____ 900

Hundreds, Tens, and Ones

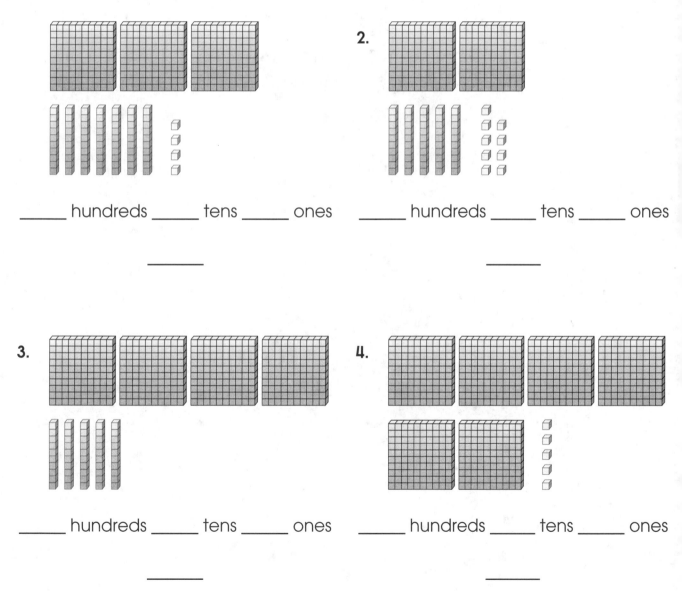

__2__ hundreds __4__ tens __6__ ones

__246__

Write how many hundreds, tens, and ones there are.
Then write the number.

_____ hundreds _____ tens _____ ones

_____

2.

_____ hundreds _____ tens _____ ones

_____

3.

_____ hundreds _____ tens _____ ones

_____

4.

_____ hundreds _____ tens _____ ones

_____

Counting by Hundreds, Tens, and Ones

Connect the dots.
Start at the ▲ and count by 100s to 900.
Start at the ● and count by 10s to 290.
Start at the ■ and count by 1s from 451 to 470.

Finding the Hundreds

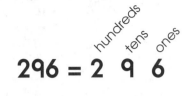

$$296 = 2 \quad 9 \quad 6$$

hundreds   tens   ones

Read the question.
Circle the correct answer.

1.	Which number shows 4 hundreds?	324	(422)	243
2.	Which number shows 2 hundreds?	280	120	342
3.	Which number shows 8 hundreds?	618	580	800
4.	Which number shows 5 hundreds?	125	251	512
5.	Which number shows 1 hundred?	180	801	810
6.	Which number shows 9 hundreds?	490	966	489
7.	Which number shows 3 hundreds?	324	833	133
8.	Which number shows 6 hundreds?	465	678	396
9.	Which number shows 7 hundreds?	700	570	897
10.	Which number shows 5 hundreds?	205	355	555
11.	Which number shows 0 hundreds?	180	510	90
12.	Which number shows 9 hundreds?	192	944	899

13. **Challenge**: Make as many numbers as you can from these digits:
    2, 5, and 8. Use one, two, or all three digits to
    make a number.

    Making more than 10
    numbers is great!

    _____

    _____

    _____

Expanded Form and Number Names

Standard form: 946

Word name: nine hundred forty six

Expanded form: 900 + 40 + 6

Write the number in expanded form.

1. 822 = _____ + _____ + _____

2. 205 = _____ + _____ + _____

3. 460 = _____ + _____ + _____

4. 743 = _____ + _____ + _____

Write the number in standard form. Then write the number name.

	standard form	number name
5. 600 + 30 + 7	_____	_____
6. 50 + 4	_____	_____
7. 900 + 0 + 1	_____	_____
8. 100 + 90 + 6	_____	_____

Compare Numbers

To compare numbers, begin at the left.
Find the first place where the digits are different.
Then compare.

> \> means greater than
> \< means less than
> = means equal to.

7 6 4
4 3 6

7 hundreds > 4 hundreds. 764 > 436

Compare the numbers. Write **<**, **>**, or **=** in the ◯.

1. 533 ◯ 427　　2. 54 ◯ 50　　3. 605 ◯ 607

4. 999 ◯ 299　　5. 724 ◯ 833　　6. 321 ◯ 321

Circle the number that is greater.

7. 256　387　　8. 467　176　　9. 52　45

10. 162　172　　11. 389　382　　12. 164　146

Circle the number that is less.

13. 234　534　　14. 898　988

15. 111　101　　16. 742　74

Adding More Numbers

$$
\begin{array}{r}
7 \\
6 \\
+\ 3 \\
\hline
16
\end{array}
$$

You can add numbers in any order.
Look for tens to make the adding easier.
$7 + 3 = 10$
Then $10 + 6 = 16$.
It's easy!

It's a snap!

Find the sum.

1.
$$
\begin{array}{r}
4 \\
3 \\
+\ 6 \\
\hline
\end{array}
$$

2.
$$
\begin{array}{r}
2 \\
7 \\
+\ 8 \\
\hline
\end{array}
$$

3.
$$
\begin{array}{r}
5 \\
6 \\
+\ 5 \\
\hline
\end{array}
$$

4.
$$
\begin{array}{r}
9 \\
4 \\
+\ 1 \\
\hline
\end{array}
$$

5.
$$
\begin{array}{r}
3 \\
8 \\
+\ 0 \\
\hline
\end{array}
$$

6.
$$
\begin{array}{r}
6 \\
8 \\
+\ 4 \\
\hline
\end{array}
$$

7.
$$
\begin{array}{r}
2 \\
3 \\
+\ 9 \\
\hline
\end{array}
$$

8.
$$
\begin{array}{r}
7 \\
1 \\
+\ 7 \\
\hline
\end{array}
$$

9.
$$
\begin{array}{r}
6 \\
2 \\
5 \\
+\ 4 \\
\hline
\end{array}
$$

10.
$$
\begin{array}{r}
7 \\
2 \\
0 \\
+\ 3 \\
\hline
\end{array}
$$

11.
$$
\begin{array}{r}
3 \\
4 \\
5 \\
+\ 6 \\
\hline
\end{array}
$$

12.
$$
\begin{array}{r}
4 \\
4 \\
4 \\
+\ 4 \\
\hline
\end{array}
$$

13. $6 + 7 + 4 = $ _____

14. $7 + 2 + 3 = $ _____

15. $8 + 5 + 2 = $ _____

16. $9 + 0 + 9 = $ _____

17. $6 + 7 + 2 + 3 = $ _____

18. $4 + 5 + 6 + 5 = $ _____

Find each sum or difference.

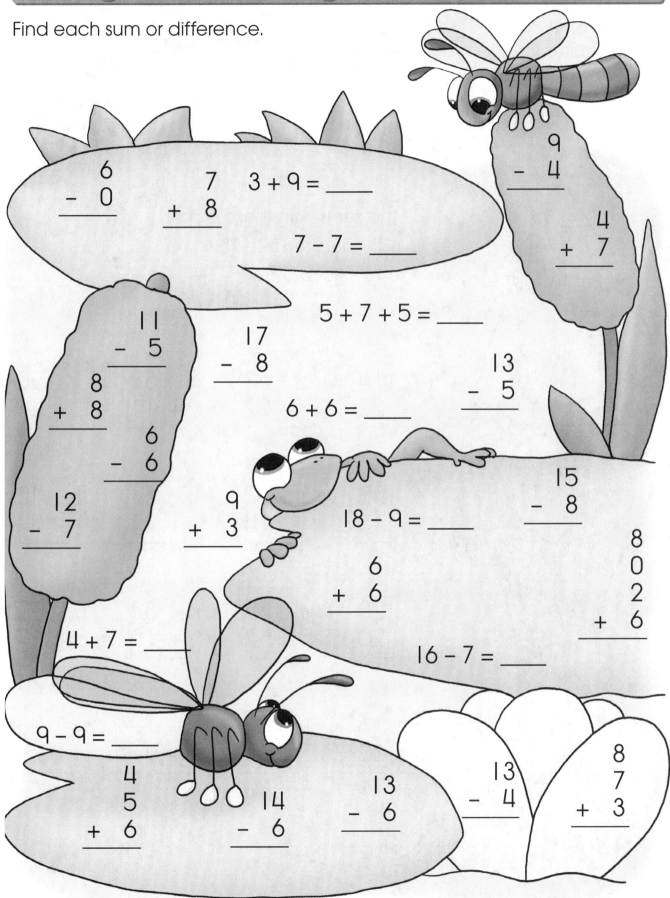

$$\begin{array}{r} 6 \\ -\ 0 \\ \hline \end{array}$$

$$\begin{array}{r} 7 \\ +\ 8 \\ \hline \end{array}$$

$3 + 9 = \underline{}$

$7 - 7 = \underline{}$

$$\begin{array}{r} 9 \\ -\ 4 \\ \hline \end{array}$$

$$\begin{array}{r} 4 \\ +\ 7 \\ \hline \end{array}$$

$5 + 7 + 5 = \underline{}$

$$\begin{array}{r} 11 \\ -\ 5 \\ \hline \end{array}$$

$$\begin{array}{r} 17 \\ -\ 8 \\ \hline \end{array}$$

$$\begin{array}{r} 13 \\ -\ 5 \\ \hline \end{array}$$

$$\begin{array}{r} 8 \\ +\ 8 \\ \hline \end{array}$$

$6 + 6 = \underline{}$

$$\begin{array}{r} 6 \\ -\ 6 \\ \hline \end{array}$$

$$\begin{array}{r} 12 \\ -\ 7 \\ \hline \end{array}$$

$$\begin{array}{r} 9 \\ +\ 3 \\ \hline \end{array}$$

$18 - 9 = \underline{}$

$$\begin{array}{r} 15 \\ -\ 8 \\ \hline \end{array}$$

$$\begin{array}{r} 6 \\ +\ 6 \\ \hline \end{array}$$

$$\begin{array}{r} 8 \\ 0 \\ +\ 2\ 6 \\ \hline \end{array}$$

$4 + 7 = \underline{}$

$16 - 7 = \underline{}$

$9 - 9 = \underline{}$

$$\begin{array}{r} 4 \\ 5 \\ +\ 6 \\ \hline \end{array}$$

$$\begin{array}{r} 14 \\ -\ 6 \\ \hline \end{array}$$

$$\begin{array}{r} 13 \\ -\ 6 \\ \hline \end{array}$$

$$\begin{array}{r} 13 \\ -\ 4 \\ \hline \end{array}$$

$$\begin{array}{r} 8 \\ 7 \\ +\ 3 \\ \hline \end{array}$$

Adding Two-Digit Numbers

Add the **ones** first.
Then add the **tens**.

70   58   76   97

49

75

37   89   40

55   87   98

88

59

69

98

Circle the **sums** with these colors:

yellow 35 – 58   **red** 59 – 75
orange 76 – 90   **brown** 91 – 99

Then color the spots on the giraffe.

1. 14
  + 23

2. 53
  + 22

3. 38
  + 11

4. 50
  + 20

5. 45
  + 13

6. 62
  + 14

7. 77
  + 21

8. 45
  + 44

9. 20
  + 20

10. 35
  + 52

11. 88
  + 10

12. 55
  + 14

13. 56
  + 32

14. 14
  + 41

15. 12
  + 47

16. 23
  + 74

*Clue: There should be 5 yellow spots, 4 **red** spots, 4 orange spots, and 3 **brown** spots.*

Partial Sum Addition

Add the **tens**.	Add the **ones**.	Add the **partial sums**.

$$\begin{array}{r} \mathbf{3}6 \\ + \ \mathbf{2}6 \\ \hline \end{array}$$
$$30 + 20 = \mathbf{50}$$

$$\begin{array}{r} 3\mathbf{6} \\ + \ 2\mathbf{6} \\ \hline 50 \\ \end{array}$$
$$6 + 6 = \mathbf{12}$$

$$\begin{array}{r} 36 \\ + \ 26 \\ \hline \mathbf{50} \\ + \ \ \mathbf{12} \\ \hline \mathbf{62} \end{array}$$ — Partial Sums

---

Find the sum.

1. $\begin{array}{r} 29 \\ + \ 23 \\ \hline \end{array}$

2. $\begin{array}{r} 17 \\ + \ 18 \\ \hline \end{array}$

3. $\begin{array}{r} 58 \\ + \ 24 \\ \hline \end{array}$

4. $\begin{array}{r} 32 \\ + \ 28 \\ \hline \end{array}$

5. $\begin{array}{r} 17 \\ + \ 43 \\ \hline \end{array}$

6. $\begin{array}{r} 57 \\ + \ 29 \\ \hline \end{array}$

7. $\begin{array}{r} 44 \\ + \ 17 \\ \hline \end{array}$

8. $\begin{array}{r} 54 \\ + \ 39 \\ \hline \end{array}$

9. $\begin{array}{r} 24 \\ + \ 26 \\ \hline \end{array}$

10. $\begin{array}{r} 15 \\ + \ 56 \\ \hline \end{array}$

11. $\begin{array}{r} 78 \\ + \ 13 \\ \hline \end{array}$

12. $\begin{array}{r} 77 \\ + \ 15 \\ \hline \end{array}$

Finding Greater Sums

When you add two-digit numbers, sometimes the sum is a three-digit number.

$$76 + 53 \over 129$$

Find the sum.

1. $\begin{array}{r} 65 \\ + 52 \\ \hline \end{array}$

2. $\begin{array}{r} 53 \\ + 56 \\ \hline \end{array}$

3. $\begin{array}{r} 47 \\ + 85 \\ \hline \end{array}$

4. $\begin{array}{r} 93 \\ + 28 \\ \hline \end{array}$

5. $\begin{array}{r} 95 \\ + 12 \\ \hline \end{array}$

6. $\begin{array}{r} 82 \\ + 28 \\ \hline \end{array}$

7. $\begin{array}{r} 63 \\ + 37 \\ \hline \end{array}$

8. $\begin{array}{r} 75 \\ + 75 \\ \hline \end{array}$

9. $\begin{array}{r} 90 \\ + 46 \\ \hline \end{array}$

10. $\begin{array}{r} 88 \\ + 88 \\ \hline \end{array}$

11. $\begin{array}{r} 91 \\ + 19 \\ \hline \end{array}$

12. $\begin{array}{r} 73 \\ + 18 \\ \hline \end{array}$

13. $\begin{array}{r} 49 \\ + 49 \\ \hline \end{array}$

14. $\begin{array}{r} 76 \\ + 45 \\ \hline \end{array}$

15. $\begin{array}{r} 57 \\ + 75 \\ \hline \end{array}$

16. $\begin{array}{r} 91 \\ + 29 \\ \hline \end{array}$

Let's add these numbers!
53 + 84 + 9

To check your answer, add the numbers in the opposite order.

$$\begin{array}{r} 53 \\ 84 \\ +9 \\ \hline 146 \end{array} \qquad \begin{array}{r} 9 \\ 84 \\ +53 \\ \hline 146 \end{array}$$

Find the sum.

1. $\begin{array}{r} 32 \\ 21 \\ +\ 15 \\ \hline \end{array}$

2. $\begin{array}{r} 63 \\ 12 \\ +\ 44 \\ \hline \end{array}$

3. $\begin{array}{r} 73 \\ 6 \\ +\ 25 \\ \hline \end{array}$

4. $\begin{array}{r} 97 \\ 98 \\ +\ 99 \\ \hline \end{array}$

5. $\begin{array}{r} 12 \\ 14 \\ 15 \\ +\ 18 \\ \hline \end{array}$

6. $\begin{array}{r} 45 \\ 21 \\ 30 \\ +\ 24 \\ \hline \end{array}$

7. $\begin{array}{r} 64 \\ 8 \\ 37 \\ +\ 40 \\ \hline \end{array}$

8. $\begin{array}{r} 56 \\ 55 \\ 4 \\ +\ 8 \\ \hline \end{array}$

9. $43 + 6 + 50 =$ _____

10. $78 + 31 + 88 =$ _____

11. $65 + 35 + 68 =$ _____

12. $37 + 8 + 39 =$ _____

13. $25 + 12 + 31 + 20 =$ _____

14. $40 + 50 + 60 + 70 =$ _____

15. $76 + 43 + 5 + 22 =$ _____

16. $25 + 35 + 45 + 55 =$ _____

Adding with Hundreds

Add the **hundreds**.	Add the **tens**.	Add the **ones**.	Add the **partial sums**.
3**0**9 + **4**73 ――――― 300 + 400 = **7**00	3**0**9 + 4**7**3 ――――― 700 0 + 70 = **70**	30**9** + 47**3** ――――― 700 70 9 + 3 = **12**	309 + 473 ――――― **700** **70** + **12** ――――― **782**

Find the sum.

1.　462
　+ 321

2.　706
　+ 132

3.　450
　+ 209

4.　456
　+ 123

5.　366
　+ 128

6.　572
　+ 309

7.　278
　+ 329

8.　293
　+ 275

9.　435
　+　48

10.　845
　+　17

11.　670
　+　45

12.　777
　+　　9

13.　352
　+ 169

14.　255
　+ 355

15.　675
　+ 125

16.　456
　+ 345

$$593 + 246 = 839$$

It's a breeze!

Find the sum.

1. $188 + 10$

2. $244 + 23$

3. $852 + 32$

4. $205 + 41$

5. $428 + 23$

6. $107 + 10$

7. $314 + 48$

8. $239 + 25$

9. $132 + 400$

10. $37 + 135$

11. $650 + 125$

12. $175 + 200$

13. $125 + 470$

14. $447 + 38$

15. $436 + 45$

16. $546 + 137$

Adding with Hundreds (2.NBT.7)

Subtracting with Hundreds

Subtract the **ones**. Regroup if needed.	Subtract the **tens**. Regroup if needed.	Subtract the **hundreds**.	Check:
$\begin{array}{r} {\scriptstyle 6\ 13} \\ 5\,7\,3 \\ -\ 2\,0\,6 \\ \hline 7 \end{array}$	$\begin{array}{r} {\scriptstyle 6\ 13} \\ 5\,7\,3 \\ -\ 2\,0\,6 \\ \hline 6\,7 \end{array}$	$\begin{array}{r} {\scriptstyle 6\ 13} \\ 5\,7\,3 \\ -\ 2\,0\,6 \\ \hline 3\,6\,7 \end{array}$	$\begin{array}{r} {\scriptstyle 1} \\ 3\,6\,7 \\ +\ 2\,0\,6 \\ \hline 5\,7\,3 \end{array}$

Find the difference. Regroup if needed.
Check your answer.

Check:

1. $\begin{array}{r} 863 \\ -\ 240 \\ \hline \end{array}$ + _____

Check:

2. $\begin{array}{r} 478 \\ -\ 435 \\ \hline \end{array}$ + _____

Check:

3. $\begin{array}{r} 573 \\ -\ 47 \\ \hline \end{array}$ + _____

Check:

4. $\begin{array}{r} 350 \\ -\ 38 \\ \hline \end{array}$ + _____

Check:

5. $\begin{array}{r} 851 \\ -\ 316 \\ \hline \end{array}$ + _____

Check:

6. $\begin{array}{r} 617 \\ -\ 395 \\ \hline \end{array}$ + _____

Find the sum or difference.

1. 534
    + 355

2. 600
    − 251

3. 162
    − 97

4. 475
    + 326

5. 982
    − 272

6. 370
    + 628

7. 103
    − 102

8. 279
    + 721

9. 516
    + 156

10. 333
    − 128

11. 1,000
    − 250

12. 827
    + 53

13. 844
    − 351

14. 100
    − 46

15. 732
    + 92

16. 657
    + 329

Measuring Inches

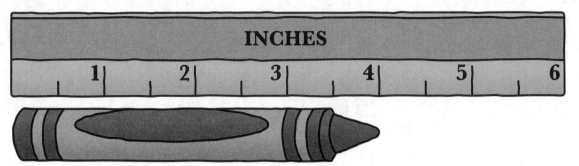

Use a ruler to measure how long something is. This ruler shows inches. To measure the crayon, put one end at the left edge of the ruler. Find the number closest to the other end.

The crayon is __4__ inches long.

Use an inch ruler to measure the objects below.

1.

The pencil is _____ inches long.

2.

The paper clip is _____ inches long.

3.

The pen is _____ inches long.

4.

The glue stick is _____ inches long.

Measuring Centimeters

CENTIMETERS

| 1 | 2 | 3 | 4 | 5 | 6 | 7 | 8 | 9 | 10 | 11 | 12 | 13 | 14 | 15 |

The ruler above shows centimeters.
A centimeter is a smaller unit of measurement than an inch.
Measure the crayon above in centimeters.

The crayon is ___10___ centimeters long.

Use an centimeter ruler to measure the objects below.

1.

The pencil is _____ centimeters long.

2.

The paper clip is _____ centimeters long.

3.

Marker

The pen is _____ centimeters long.

4.

GLUE

The glue stick is _____ centimeters long.

Measuring Length

INCHES	CENTIMETERS
1 2 3	1 2 3 4 5 6 7 8

You can measure how long something is using different units of measurement.

The paper clip is about 1 inch long and about 3 centimeters long.

You can measure bigger things in feet, yards, and meters.

$$12 \text{ inches} = 1 \text{ foot}$$
$$3 \text{ feet} = 1 \text{ yard}$$
$$100 \text{ centimeters} = 1 \text{ meter}$$

Fill in the blanks.

1.

The chalkboard is _____ feet long.

The chalkboard is about _____ meters long.

2.

The hose is _____ yards long.

The hose is about _____ meters long.

Read and solve each word problem.

1. Ms. Green has a garden that is 10 feet long.
   She added 2 more feet to the garden.
   How long is her garden now?

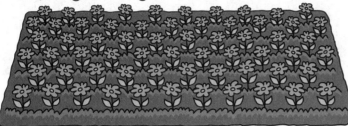

Solve

_____

◯ _____

_____ feet

2. A garden flower was 13 centimeters tall.
   Then it grew 6 more centimeters.
   How many centimeters tall is the flower now?

Solve

_____

◯ _____

_____ centimeters

3. Another flower was 9 inches tall.
   Ms. Green cut off 6 inches of the flower.
   How tall is the flower now?

Solve

_____

◯ _____

_____ inches

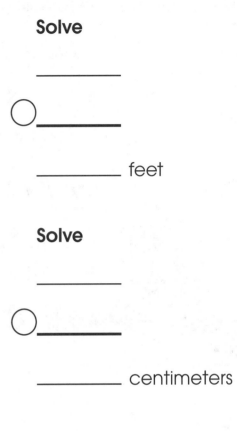

4. A tree was 20 feet tall.
   A strong wind broke 5 feet off the top.
   How tall is the tree now?

Solve

_____

◯ _____

_____ feet

A number line is similar to a ruler.
Use a number line to help you add or subtract.

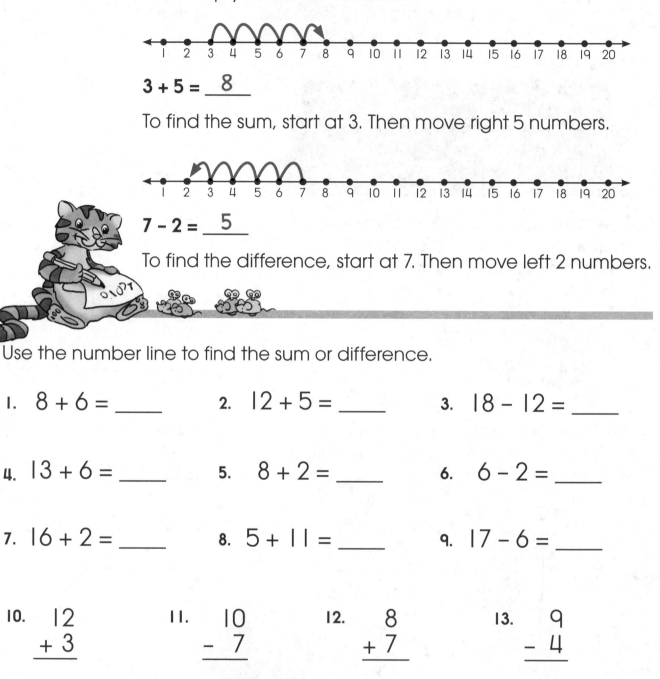

$3 + 5 =$ ___8___

To find the sum, start at 3. Then move right 5 numbers.

$7 - 2 =$ ___5___

To find the difference, start at 7. Then move left 2 numbers.

Use the number line to find the sum or difference.

1. $8 + 6 =$ ____   2. $12 + 5 =$ ____   3. $18 - 12 =$ ____

4. $13 + 6 =$ ____   5. $8 + 2 =$ ____   6. $6 - 2 =$ ____

7. $16 + 2 =$ ____   8. $5 + 11 =$ ____   9. $17 - 6 =$ ____

10.
$$\begin{array}{r} 12 \\ + 3 \\ \hline \end{array}$$

11.
$$\begin{array}{r} 10 \\ - 7 \\ \hline \end{array}$$

12.
$$\begin{array}{r} 8 \\ + 7 \\ \hline \end{array}$$

13.
$$\begin{array}{r} 9 \\ - 4 \\ \hline \end{array}$$

14.
$$\begin{array}{r} 19 \\ - 12 \\ \hline \end{array}$$

15.
$$\begin{array}{r} 15 \\ + 5 \\ \hline \end{array}$$

16.
$$\begin{array}{r} 17 \\ - 6 \\ \hline \end{array}$$

17.
$$\begin{array}{r} 15 \\ + 2 \\ \hline \end{array}$$

Use a number line to find differences.

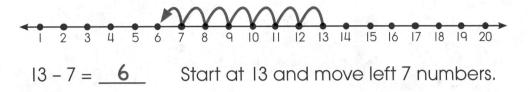

$13 - 7 = \underline{\quad 6 \quad}$ Start at 13 and move left 7 numbers.

Use the number line to find the difference.

1. $\begin{array}{r} 20 \\ -17 \\ \hline \end{array}$
2. $\begin{array}{r} 19 \\ -4 \\ \hline \end{array}$
3. $\begin{array}{r} 15 \\ -14 \\ \hline \end{array}$
4. $\begin{array}{r} 8 \\ -3 \\ \hline \end{array}$
5. $\begin{array}{r} 20 \\ -6 \\ \hline \end{array}$

6. $\begin{array}{r} 12 \\ -5 \\ \hline \end{array}$
7. $\begin{array}{r} 13 \\ -8 \\ \hline \end{array}$
8. $\begin{array}{r} 11 \\ -8 \\ \hline \end{array}$
9. $\begin{array}{r} 16 \\ -7 \\ \hline \end{array}$
10. $\begin{array}{r} 9 \\ -2 \\ \hline \end{array}$

11. $\begin{array}{r} 10 \\ -3 \\ \hline \end{array}$
12. $\begin{array}{r} 13 \\ -6 \\ \hline \end{array}$
13. $\begin{array}{r} 9 \\ -1 \\ \hline \end{array}$
14. $\begin{array}{r} 14 \\ -8 \\ \hline \end{array}$
15. $\begin{array}{r} 10 \\ -6 \\ \hline \end{array}$

16. $\begin{array}{r} 11 \\ -2 \\ \hline \end{array}$
17. $\begin{array}{r} 19 \\ -13 \\ \hline \end{array}$
18. $\begin{array}{r} 17 \\ -4 \\ \hline \end{array}$
19. $\begin{array}{r} 13 \\ -5 \\ \hline \end{array}$
20. $\begin{array}{r} 15 \\ -8 \\ \hline \end{array}$

Which Number Is Missing?

Find the missing number. Use the number line if you need help.

1. $\begin{array}{r} 11 \\ -\ 2 \\ \hline \boxed{} \end{array}$

2. $\begin{array}{r} 7 \\ -\ 4 \\ \hline \boxed{} \end{array}$

3. $\begin{array}{r} 12 \\ -\ \boxed{} \\ \hline 8 \end{array}$

4. $\begin{array}{r} 11 \\ -\ 7 \\ \hline \boxed{} \end{array}$

5. $\begin{array}{r} 9 \\ -\ 5 \\ \hline \boxed{} \end{array}$

6. $\begin{array}{r} \boxed{} \\ -\ 2 \\ \hline 5 \end{array}$

7. $\begin{array}{r} 12 \\ -\ 7 \\ \hline \boxed{} \end{array}$

8. $\begin{array}{r} 10 \\ -\ 3 \\ \hline \boxed{} \end{array}$

9. $\begin{array}{r} 10 \\ -\ 8 \\ \hline \boxed{} \end{array}$

10. $\begin{array}{r} 11 \\ -\ 3 \\ \hline \boxed{} \end{array}$

11. $\begin{array}{r} 11 \\ -\ 8 \\ \hline \boxed{} \end{array}$

12. $\begin{array}{r} 9 \\ -\ 3 \\ \hline \boxed{} \end{array}$

13. $\begin{array}{r} 8 \\ -\ \boxed{} \\ \hline 5 \end{array}$

14. $\begin{array}{r} 7 \\ -\ \boxed{} \\ \hline 4 \end{array}$

15. $\begin{array}{r} \boxed{} \\ -\ 6 \\ \hline 4 \end{array}$

16. $\begin{array}{r} \boxed{} \\ -\ 5 \\ \hline 5 \end{array}$

A clock tells the time. It shows 12 hours. Each hour has 60 minutes. A clock face has two hands.

The short hand, or hour hand, points to the hours. The long hand, or minute hand, points to the minutes. When the long hand points to 12, it is at the beginning of the hour.

This clock face shows 8 o'clock. A digital clock says the same time: 8:00.

Write the times on the digital clocks.
Draw hands on the clock faces.

1. 6 o'clock

2. 7 o'clock

3. 4 o'clock

4. 9 o'clock

Telling Time to the Half Hour

An hour has 60 minutes. There are 5 minutes between each number on a clock face.

At the 6, thirty minutes have passed. It is halfway between one hour and the next.

The minute hand (long hand) points to the 6.

The hour hand (short hand) is halfway between one hour and the next one.

This clock shows eight thirty or 8:30. You can also say "half past 8."

Fill in the blanks. Then draw hands on the clock face and write the time on the digital clocks.

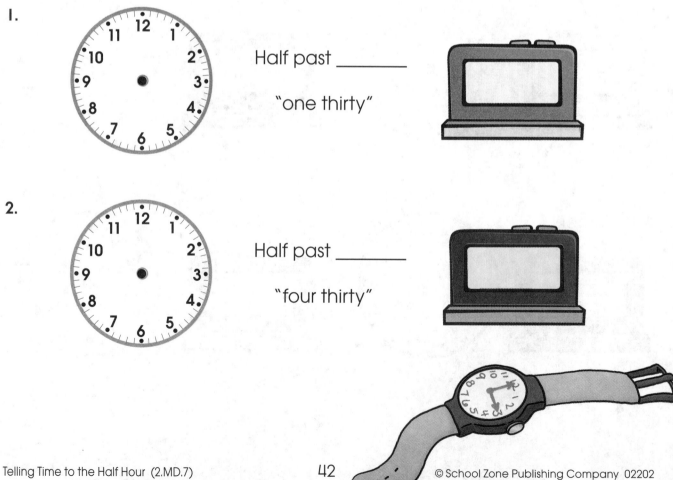

1.

Half past _____

"one thirty"

2.

Half past _____

"four thirty"

On a clock face, there are five minutes between each number.

If the minute hand points to the 3, it means 15 minutes past the hour.

Look at each clock face. Write the time it shows.

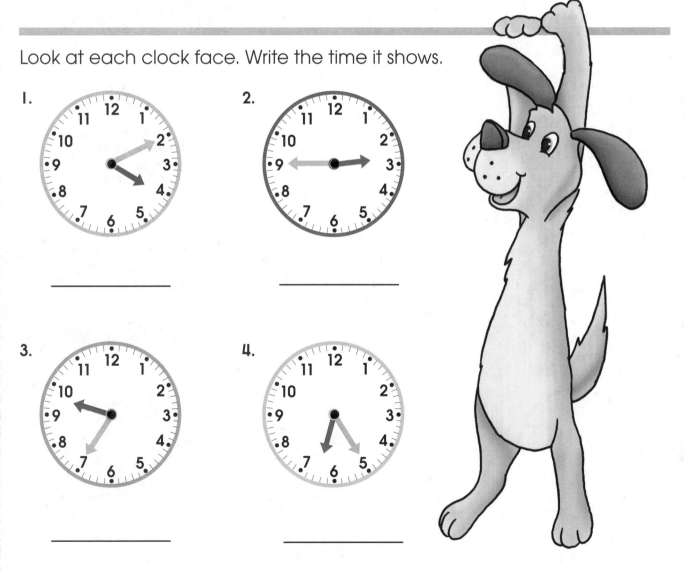

1.

_____

2.

_____

3.

_____

4.

_____

Telling Time with a.m. and p.m.

A clock shows 12 hours, but a day has 24 hours.

From 12:00 midnight to 12:00 noon are a.m. hours. They are morning hours.

From 12:00 noon to 12:00 midnight are p.m. hours. They are afternoon and evening hours.

Read the time. Circle **a.m.** or **p.m.** Then draw the hands on the clock face and write the time on the digital clock.

1. Time for breakfast:
   7:15   a.m.   p.m.

2. Time to go to bed:
   8:30   a.m.   p.m.

3. School is out for the day:
   3:40   a.m.   p.m.

4. Line up for lunch:
   11:20   a.m.   p.m.

Word Problems with Money

These coins have a value in cents (¢).

Look at the pictures. Then solve each problem.

1. Fred bought a [balloon]   _____ ¢

   and a [crayon]   + _____ ¢

   How much did he spend?   _____ ¢

2. Gina bought a [whistle]   _____ ¢

   and a [lollipop]   + _____ ¢

   How much did she spend?   _____ ¢

3. Lauren had [dime] [nickel]   _____ ¢

   She bought a [whistle]   − _____ ¢

   How much did she have left?   _____ ¢

© School Zone Publishing Company 02202

Word Problems with Money (2.MD.8)

= 1¢   = 5¢   = 10¢   = 25¢

Look at the pictures. Then solve each problem.

1. Rachel had a dime.   _____ ¢

   She bought a   − _____ ¢

   How much did she have left?   _____ ¢

2. Will bought a   _____ ¢

   and a   + _____ ¢

   How much did he spend?   _____ ¢

3. Kent bought an   _____ ¢

   and an   + _____ ¢

   How much did he spend?   _____ ¢

Buying with Money

These kids each want to buy 2 things. Solve the problems by finding what they can buy without any money left over. The first one is done for you.

1. Ted has 18¢.
What two things can he buy?

bank	12 ¢
ball	+ 6 ¢
	18 ¢

2. Sheena has 22¢.
What two things can she buy?

_____	_____ ¢
_____	+ _____ ¢
	_____ ¢

3. Sam has 21¢.
What two things can he buy?

_____	_____ ¢
_____	+ _____ ¢
	_____ ¢

4. Patty has 19¢.
What two things can she buy?

_____	_____ ¢
_____	+ _____ ¢
	_____ ¢

5. Vera has 25¢.
What two things can she buy?

_____	_____ ¢
_____	+ _____ ¢
	_____ ¢

6. Greg has 17¢.
What two things can he buy?

_____	_____ ¢
_____	+ _____ ¢
	_____ ¢

= 1¢   = 5¢   = 10¢   = 25¢

Solve each problem, and circle the correct answer.

1. Emily has 2 nickels and 2 dimes.
   She has _____.

   4¢   12¢   20¢   30¢

2. Miguel has 1 quarter and 1 penny.
   He has _____.

   21¢   26¢   30¢   31¢

3. Mr. Baker has 1 quarter, 1 dime, and 2 nickels.
   He has _____.

   22¢   32¢   45¢   55¢

4. Kara has 5 dimes, 3 nickels, and 2 pennies.
   She has _____.

   17¢   22¢   67¢   82¢

5. Rob had 2 quarters and 3 pennies.
   He spent 25¢.
   Now, Rob has _____.

   13¢   28¢   53¢   78¢

6. Jill had 1 quarter, 3 dimes, and 4 pennies.
   She spent 2 dimes.
   Now, Jill has _____.

   39¢   59¢   69¢   79¢

Using Dollars

One dollar ($1.00) is the same as 100 pennies (100¢).

100 pennies = 20 nickels = 10 dimes = 4 quarters = 1 dollar

Solve each problem. The first one is done for you.

1. Ben has 2 dollars, 4 dimes, and 7 pennies.

Ben has __$2.00__ and __47¢__ .

2. Mindy has 3 dollars, 5 nickels, and 3 pennies.

Mindy has _____ and _____ .

3. Stuart has 4 dollars, 3 dimes, and 3 nickels.

Stuart has _____ and _____ .

4. Val has 1 dollar, 2 quarters, and 9 pennies.

Val has _____ and _____ .

5. Dana had 2 dollars and 65¢. She spent 1 dollar and 40¢. How much money does she have left?

Dana has _____ and _____ .

6. Luke had 2 dollars and 12¢. His dad gave him 75¢. How much money does he have in all?

Luke has _____ and _____ .

7. Maria had 5 dollars and 55¢. Her mom gave her 2 dollars and 25¢. How much money does she have in all?

Maria has _____ and _____ .

8. Owen had 6 dollars and 93¢. He spent 4 dollars and 37¢. How much money does he have left?

Owen has _____ and _____ .

Using a Picture Graph

Some kids are collecting seashells.
Use the picture graph to answer the questions.

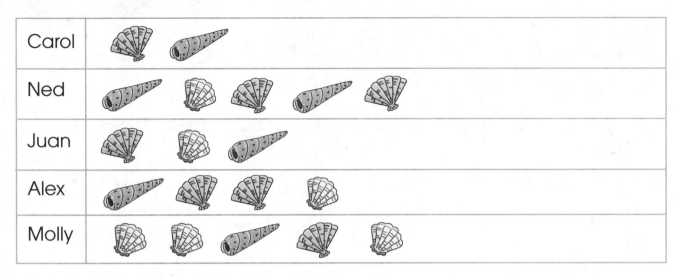

Carol	
Ned	
Juan	
Alex	
Molly	

1. How many shells does Carol have? _____

2. How many shells does Ned have? _____

3. How many shells does Juan have? _____

4. How many shells does Alex have? _____

5. How many shells does Molly have? _____

6. How many shells do Ned and Molly have in all?
   Write a number sentence to show the problem.

   _____ + _____ = _____

7. How many shells did the kids collect in all?
   Write a number sentence to show the problem.

   _____ + _____ + _____ + _____ + _____ = _____

Using a Picture Graph

Someone gave these dogs a lot of bones.
Use the picture graph to answer the questions.

Spot	🦴 🦴 🦴
Buddy	🦴 🦴 🦴
Angel	🦴 🦴 🦴 🦴 🦴
Lucky	🦴 🦴
Trixie	🦴 🦴 🦴 🦴

1. How many bones does Buddy have? _____

2. How many bones does Lucky have? _____

3. How many bones does Trixie have? _____

4. Which dog has the most bones? _____

5. Which dog has the fewest bones? _____

6. How many bones do Angel and Trixie have altogether?
   Write a number sentence to show the problem.

   _____ + _____ = _____

7. How many bones do Buddy, Angel, and Lucky have in all?
   Write a number sentence to show the problem.

   _____ + _____ + _____ = _____

Using a Picture Graph

Some kids were counting butterflies in the butterfly garden. Use the picture graph to answer the questions. Use the **+** and **–** when needed.

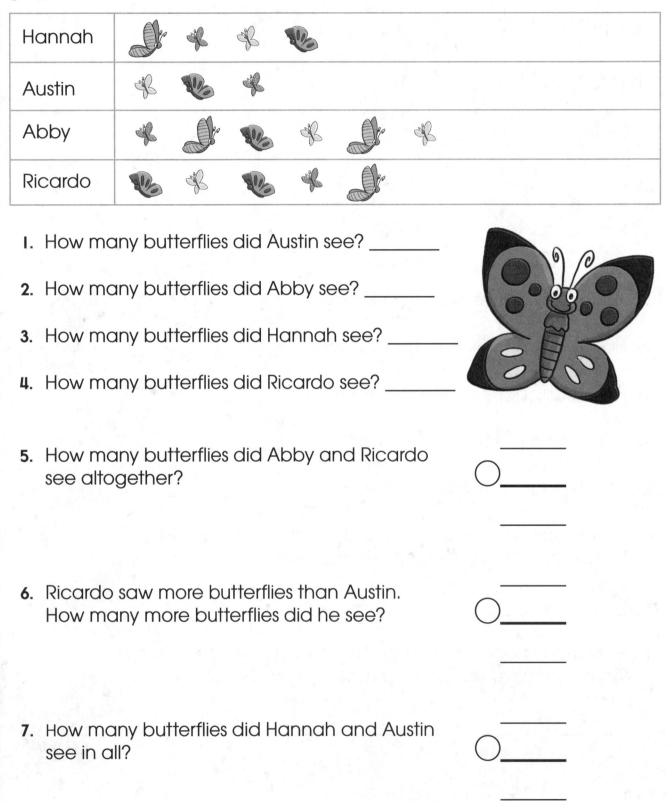

Hannah				
Austin				
Abby				
Ricardo				

1. How many butterflies did Austin see? _____

2. How many butterflies did Abby see? _____

3. How many butterflies did Hannah see? _____

4. How many butterflies did Ricardo see? _____

5. How many butterflies did Abby and Ricardo see altogether?

   ◯ _____
   _____

6. Ricardo saw more butterflies than Austin. How many more butterflies did he see?

   _____
   ◯ _____
   _____

7. How many butterflies did Hannah and Austin see in all?

   _____
   ◯ _____
   _____

Using a Bar Graph

Some kids read books during Library Week.
Use the bar graph to answer each question below.

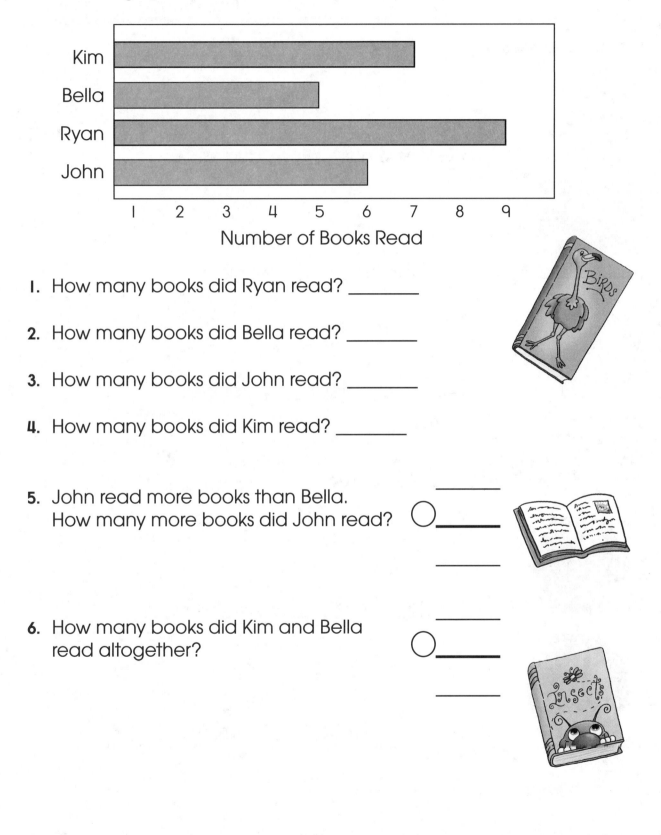

Number of Books Read

1. How many books did Ryan read? _____

2. How many books did Bella read? _____

3. How many books did John read? _____

4. How many books did Kim read? _____

5. John read more books than Bella.
   How many more books did John read? ◯ _____

6. How many books did Kim and Bella
   read altogether? ◯ _____

Using a Bar Graph (2.MD.10)

Looking at Shapes

Two sides of a shape meet to form an angle.

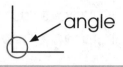

Fill in each blank.

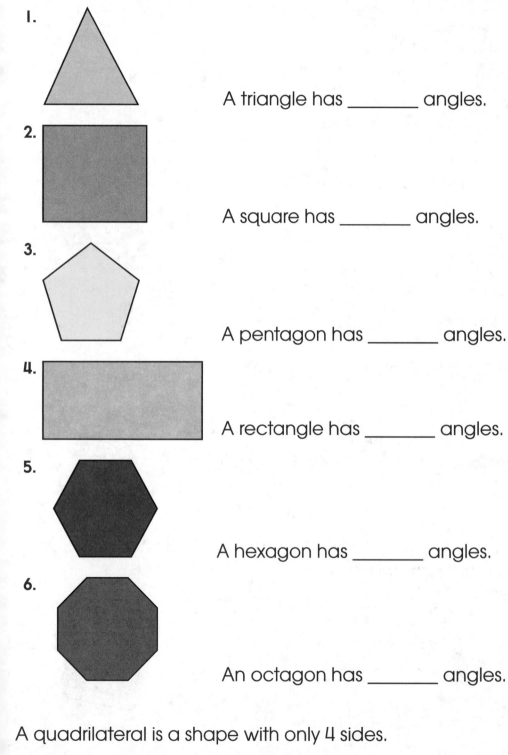

1.

A triangle has _____ angles.

2.

A square has _____ angles.

3.

A pentagon has _____ angles.

4.

A rectangle has _____ angles.

5.

A hexagon has _____ angles.

6.

An octagon has _____ angles.

A quadrilateral is a shape with only 4 sides.

7. Which shapes above are quadrilaterals? _____

Shapes can be measured in equal units.
Count the square units in the rectangles below.

1.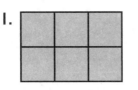

The rectangle is _____ square units across.

The rectangle is _____ square units down.

The rectangle has _____ square units in all.

2.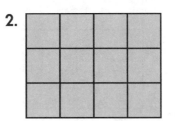

The rectangle is _____ square units across.

The rectangle is _____ square units down.

The rectangle has _____ square units in all.

3.

The rectangle is _____ square units across.

The rectangle is _____ square units down.

The rectangle has _____ square units in all.

4.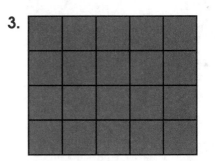

The rectangle is _____ square units across.

The rectangle is _____ square units down.

The rectangle has _____ square units in all.

Looking for Equal Parts

Shapes can be divided into any number of parts.
Equal parts are the same size and shape.

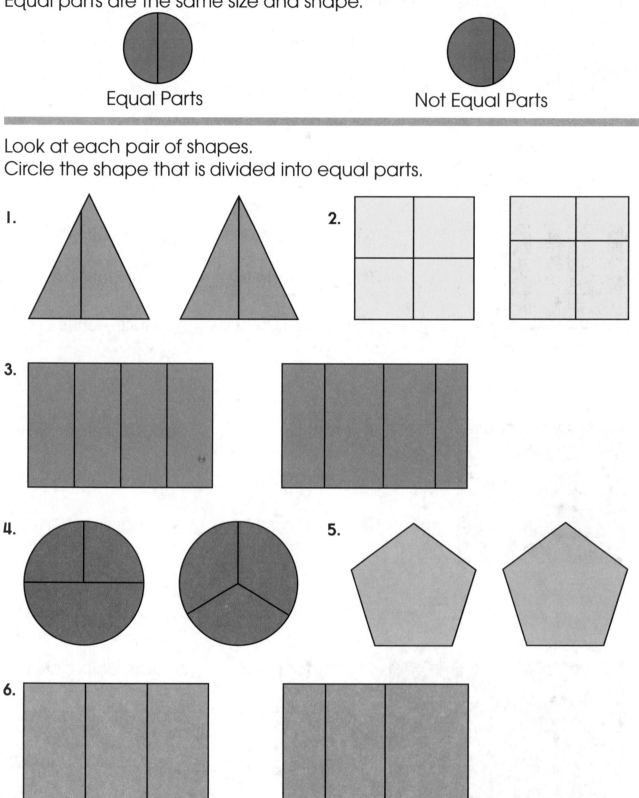

Equal Parts

Not Equal Parts

Look at each pair of shapes.
Circle the shape that is divided into equal parts.

1.

2.

3.

4.

5.

6.

Seeing Halves

When a shape is divided into 2 equal parts, each part is one-half or $\frac{1}{2}$ of the shape.
$\frac{1}{2}$ is a fraction.

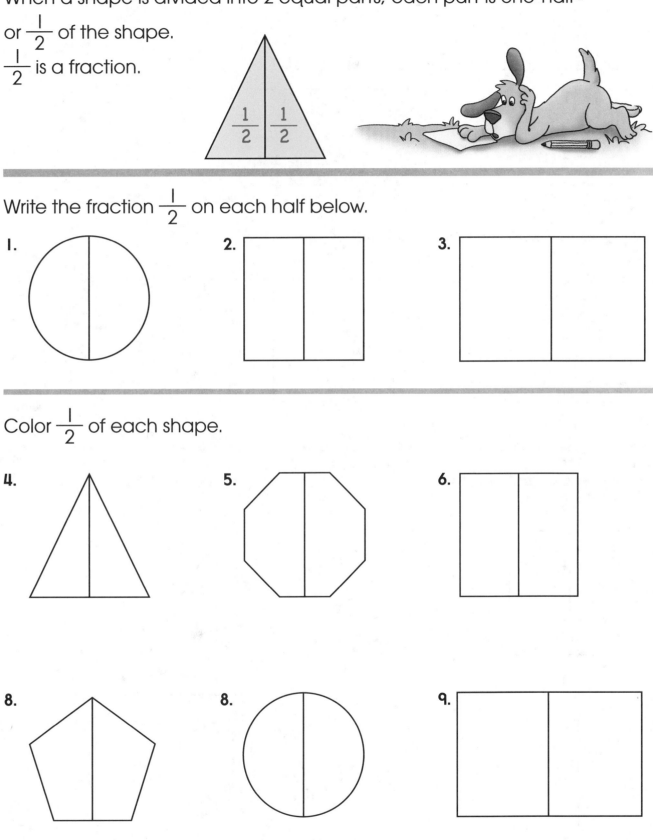

Write the fraction $\frac{1}{2}$ on each half below.

1.

2.

3.

Color $\frac{1}{2}$ of each shape.

4.

5.

6.

8.

8.

9.

Seeing Thirds

When a shape is divided into 3 equal parts, each part is one-third or $\frac{1}{3}$ of the shape.

Two parts of the same shape are two-thirds or $\frac{2}{3}$.

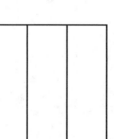

Write the fraction $\frac{1}{3}$ on each third below.

1.

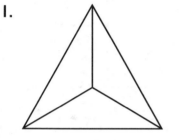

2.

3.

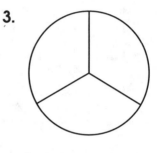

Color $\frac{1}{3}$ of each shape.

4.

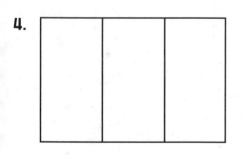

5.

6.

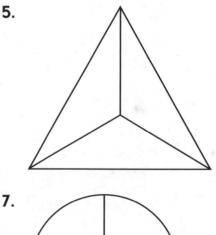

7.

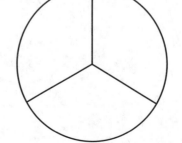

Seeing Fourths

When a shape is divided into 4 equal parts, each part is one-fourth or $\frac{1}{4}$ of the shape.

The whole shape has four-fourths or $\frac{4}{4}$.

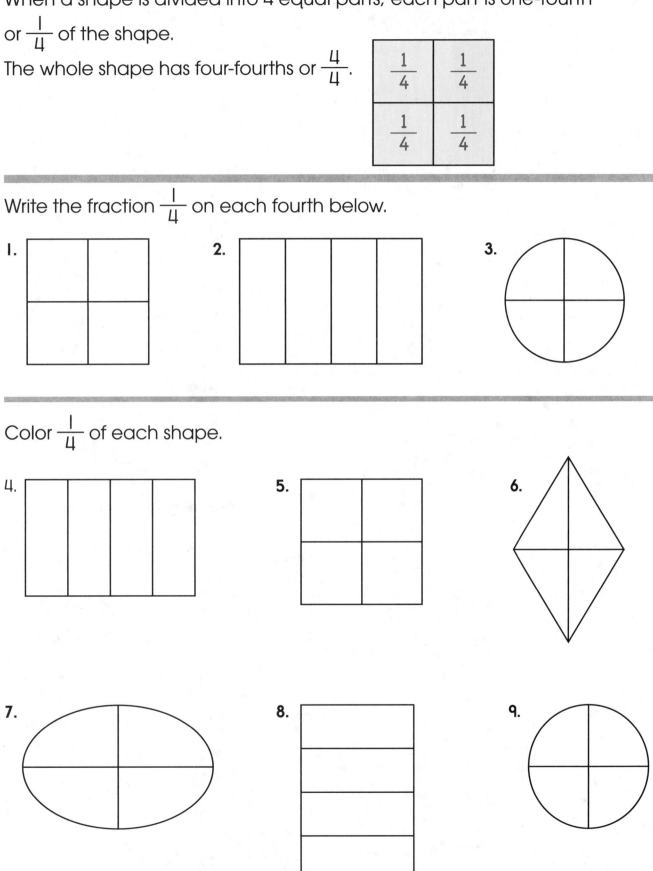

Write the fraction $\frac{1}{4}$ on each fourth below.

1.

2.

3.

Color $\frac{1}{4}$ of each shape.

4.

5.

6.

7.

8.

9.

Understanding Fractions (2.G.3)

Answer Key

Page 1
1. 3 + 5 = 8 fish in all
2. 2 + 4 = 6 apples in all
3. 6 + 3 = 9 flowers in all

Page 2
1. 8 - 4 = 4 butterflies left
2. 7 - 2 = 5 cars left
3. 7 - 4 = 3 leaves left

Page 3
1.
$$\begin{array}{r} 7 \\ -\ 3 \\ \hline 4 \text{ cookies} \end{array}$$
2.
$$\begin{array}{r} 5 \\ +\ 3 \\ \hline 8 \text{ cats} \end{array}$$

Page 4
1.
$$\begin{array}{r} 7 \\ +\ 4 \\ \hline 11 \text{ crayons} \end{array}$$
2.
$$\begin{array}{r} 2 \\ +\ 8 \\ \hline 10 \text{ turtles} \end{array}$$
3.
$$\begin{array}{r} 12 \\ -\ 7 \\ \hline 5 \text{ pears} \end{array}$$

Page 5
1. 9   2. 7   3. 8
4. 8   5. 9   6. 10
7. 9   8. 10   9. 10
10. 10; 3 + 7 = 10

Page 6
1. 5 + 9 = 14   2. 9 + 6 = 15   3. 7 + 6 = 13
   9 + 5 = 14   6 + 9 = 15   6 + 7 = 13
   14 - 5 = 9   15 - 6 = 9   13 - 6 = 7
   14 - 9 = 5   15 - 9 = 6   13 - 7 = 6

4. 8 + 9 = 17   5. 8 + 6 = 14   6. 7 + 9 = 16
   9 + 8 = 17   6 + 8 = 14   9 + 7 = 16
   17 - 8 = 9   14 - 6 = 8   16 - 7 = 9
   17 - 9 = 8   14 - 8 = 6   16 - 9 = 7

Page 7
1. 12, 12, 7, 5
2. 5, 5
3. 6, 9, 6, 6
4. 12, 12
5. 11, 5, 5, 5
6. 4, 11, 4, 11

Page 8
1. 4, 4   2. 6, 6   3. 9, 3
4. 6, 7   5. 7, 8   6. 9, 9
7. 7, 7   8. 7, 7   9. 9, 6
10. 6, 6   11. 9, 8   12. 5, 8

Page 9
13, 12, 7
8, 13, 9
12, 9, 9
8, 14, 15
16, 17, 5
SECRETARY
BIRD

Page 10
Set A has more correct answers.

Set A
15, 12
6, 8 (9)
14 (15), 13
9, 8 (9)

Set B
13, 14 (16)
6 (7), 8
12, 13 (14)
7 (8), 9

Page 11
1. 9 = 2 + 2 + 2 + 2 + 1; odd
2. 8 = 2 + 2 + 2 + 2; even
3. 10 = 2 + 2 + 2 + 2 + 2; even
4. 2, 4, 6, 8, 10, 12, 14, 16, 18, 20
5. 1, 3, 5, 7, 9, 11, 13, 15, 17, 19

Page 12

Page 13
1.
$$\begin{array}{r} 4 \\ +4 \\ +4 \\ \hline 12 \end{array}$$
2.
$$\begin{array}{r} 5 \\ +5 \\ +5 \\ +5 \\ \hline 20 \end{array}$$
3.
$$\begin{array}{r} 4 \\ +4 \\ +4 \\ +4 \\ \hline 16 \end{array}$$
4.
$$\begin{array}{r} 2 \\ +2 \\ +2 \\ \hline 6 \end{array}$$
5.
$$\begin{array}{r} 5 \\ +5 \\ \hline 10 \end{array}$$
6.
$$\begin{array}{r} 3 \\ +3 \\ +3 \\ \hline 9 \end{array}$$

Page 14
1.
$$\begin{array}{r} 2 \\ +2 \\ +2 \\ +2 \\ \hline 8 \end{array}$$
2.
$$\begin{array}{r} 5 \\ +5 \\ +5 \\ +5 \\ +5 \\ \hline 25 \end{array}$$
3.
$$\begin{array}{r} 4 \\ +4 \\ \hline 8 \end{array}$$
4.
$$\begin{array}{r} 3 \\ +3 \\ \hline 6 \end{array}$$
5.
$$\begin{array}{r} 3 \\ +3 \\ +3 \\ \hline 9 \end{array}$$
6.
$$\begin{array}{r} 5 \\ +5 \\ +5 \\ \hline 15 \end{array}$$

Page 15
1. 3 2, 32
2. 2 9, 29
3. 8 7, 87
4. 4 0, 40
5. 9 4, 94

Page 16
1. 3 2, 32
2. 2 9, 29
3. 1 6, 16
4. 4 0, 40
5. 7 3, 73

Page 17
1. 4 hundreds = 400
2. 6 hundreds = 600
3. 8 hundreds = 800
4. 5 hundreds = 500

Page 18
100
200
300
400
500
600
700
800
900

300, 500, 700, 900
200, 400, 500, 700, 800

Page 19
1. 3 hundreds   7 tens   4 ones
   374
2. 2 hundreds   5 tens   9 ones
   259
3. 4 hundreds   5 tens   0 ones
   450
4. 6 hundreds   0 tens   5 ones
   605

Page 20

Page 21

1. 422 **13.** 2, 5, 8, 25, 28,
2. 280   52, 58, 82, 85,
3. 800   258, 285, 528,
4. 512   582, 825, 852
5. 180
6. 966
7. 324
8. 678
9. 700
10. 555
11. 90
12. 944

Page 22

1. 800 + 20 + 2
2. 200 + 0 + 5
3. 400 + 60 + 0
4. 700 + 40 + 3
5. 637 six hundred thirty seven
6. 54 fifty four
7. 901 nine hundred one
8. 196 one hundred ninety six

Page 23

1. 533 > 427   2. 54 > 50   3. 605 < 607
4. 999 > 299   5. 724 < 833   6. 321 = 321
7. 387   8. 467   9. 52
10. 172   11. 389   12. 164
13. 234   14. 898
15. 101   16. 74

Page 24

1. 13   2. 17   3. 16   4. 14
5. 11   6. 18   7. 14   8. 15
9. 17   10. 12   11. 18   12. 16
13. 17   14. 12
15. 15   16. 18
17. 18   18. 20

Page 25

$$6 - 0 = 6$$
$$7 + 8 = 15$$
$$3 + 9 = 12$$
$$7 - 7 = 0$$
$$9 - 4 = 5$$
$$4 + 7 = 11$$
$$5 + 7 + 5 = 17$$
$$11 - 5 = 6$$
$$17 - 8 = 9$$
$$13 - 5 = 8$$
$$8 + 8 = 16$$
$$6 - 6 = 0$$
$$6 + 6 = 12$$
$$12 - 7 = 5$$
$$9 + 3 = 12$$
$$18 - 9 = 9$$
$$15 - 8 = 7$$
$$6 + 6 = 12$$
$$8 + 0 + 2 + 6 = 16$$
$$4 + 7 = 11$$
$$16 - 7 = 9$$
$$9 - 9 = 0$$
$$4 + 5 + 6 = 15$$
$$14 - 6 = 8$$
$$13 - 6 = 7$$
$$13 - 4 = 9$$
$$8 + 7 + 3 = 18$$

Page 26

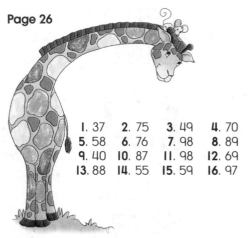

1. 37   2. 75   3. 49   4. 70
5. 58   6. 76   7. 98   8. 89
9. 40   10. 87   11. 98   12. 69
13. 88   14. 55   15. 59   16. 97

Page 27

1. 52   2. 35   3. 82   4. 60
5. 60   6. 86   7. 61   8. 93
9. 50   10. 71   11. 91   12. 92

Page 28

1. 117   2. 109   3. 132   4. 121
5. 107   6. 110   7. 100   8. 150
9. 136   10. 176   11. 110   12. 91
13. 98   14. 121   15. 132   16. 120

Page 29

1. 68   2. 119   3. 104   4. 294
5. 59   6. 120   7. 149   8. 123
9. 99   10. 197
11. 168   12. 84
13. 88   14. 220
15. 146   16. 160

Page 30

1. 783   2. 838   3. 659   4. 579
5. 494   6. 881   7. 607   8. 568
9. 483   10. 862   11. 715   12. 786
13. 521   14. 610   15. 800   16. 801

Page 31

1. 198   2. 267   3. 884   4. 246
5. 451   6. 117   7. 362   8. 264
9. 532   10. 172   11. 775   12. 375
13. 595   14. 485   15. 481   16. 683

Page 32

1. 623   2. 43
3. 526   4. 312
5. 535   6. 222

Page 33

1. 889   2. 349   3. 65   4. 801
5. 710   6. 998   7. 1   8. 1000
9. 672   10. 205   11. 750   12. 880
13. 493   14. 54   15. 824   16. 986

Page 34

1. 5
2. 2
3. 6
4. 3

Page 35

1. 13
2. 5
3. 15
4. 7

Page 36

1. 7, 2
2. 10, 9

Answer Key

Page 37

1. 10
    + 2
    ————
    12 feet

2. 13
    + 6
    ————
    19 centimeters

3.   9
    − 6
    ————
     3 inches

4. 20
    − 5
    ————
    15 feet

Page 38

1. 14   2. 17   3. 6
4. 19   5. 10   6. 4
7. 18   8. 16   9. 11
10. 15 11. 3   12. 15 13. 5
14. 7   15. 20 16. 11 17. 17

Page 39

1. 3   2. 15   3. 1   4. 5   5. 14
6. 7   7. 5   8. 3   9. 9   10. 7
11. 7   12. 7   13. 8   14. 6   15. 4
16. 9   17. 6   18. 13 19. 8   20. 7

Page 40

1. 9   2. 3   3. 4   4. 4
5. 4   6. 7   7. 5   8. 7
9. 2   10. 8   11. 3   12. 6
13. 3   14. 3   15. 10 16. 10

Page 41

1. 6:00
2. 7:00
3. 4:00
4. 9:00

Page 42

1. Half past 1   1:30
2. Half past 4   4:30

Page 43

1. 4:10
2. 2:45
3. 9:35
4. 6:25

Page 44

1. 7:15 a.m.   7:15
2. 8:30 p.m.   8:30
3. 3:40 p.m.   3:40
4. 11:20 a.m.   11:20

Page 45

1.   5¢
    + 3¢
    ————
     8¢

2.   6¢
    + 7¢
    ————
    13¢

3. 15¢
    − 6¢
    ————
     9¢

Page 46

1. 10¢
    − 7¢
    ————
     3¢

2.   9¢
    + 12¢
    ————
    21¢

3.   8¢
    + 10¢
    ————
    18¢

Page 47

1. bank   12¢
   ball   + 6¢
             ————
              18¢

2. book   10¢
   bank   + 12¢
             ————
              22¢

3. book   10¢
   dog   + 11¢
             ————
              21¢

4. doll   13¢
   ball   + 6¢
             ————
              19¢

5. doll   13¢
   bank   + 12¢
             ————
              25¢

6. ball   6¢
   dog   + 11¢
             ————
              17¢

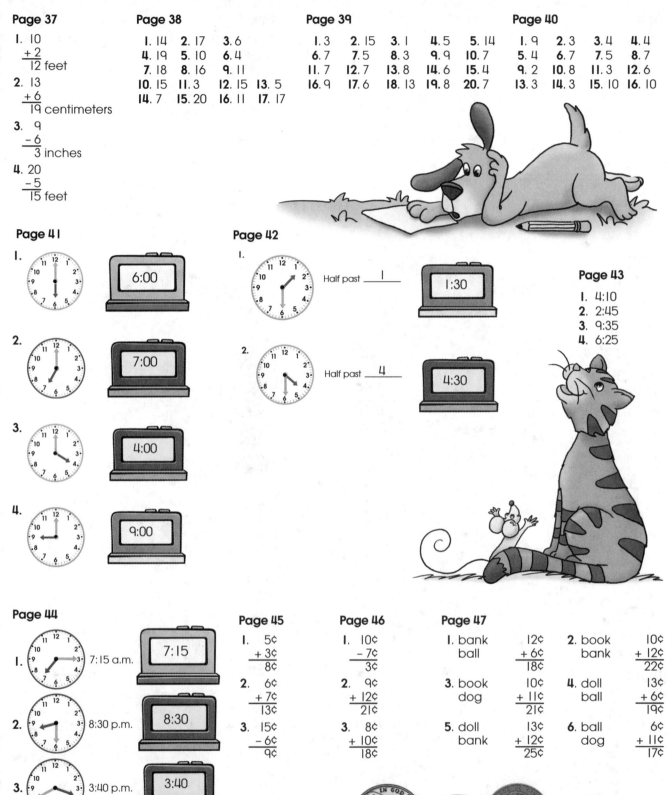

Page 48
1. 30¢
2. 26¢
3. 45¢
4. 67¢
5. 28¢
6. 39¢

Page 49
1. $2.00, 47¢
2. $3.00, 28¢
3. $4.00, 45¢
4. $1.00, 59¢
5. $1.00, 25¢
6. $2.00, 87¢
7. $7.00, 80¢

Page 50
1. 2
2. 5
3. 3
4. 4
5. 5
6. 5 + 5 = 10
7. 2 + 5 + 3 + 4 + 5 = 19

Page 51
1. 3
2. 2
3. 4
4. Angel
5. Lucky
6. 5 + 4 = 9
7. 3 + 5 + 2 = 10

Page 52
1. 3
2. 6
3. 4
4. 5
5. 6 + 5 = 11
6. 5 - 3 = 2
7. 4 + 3 = 7
8. 6 - 4 = 2

Page 53
1. 9
2. 5
3. 6
4. 7
5. 6 - 5 = 1
6. 7 + 5 = 12

Page 54
1. 3
2. 4
3. 5
4. 4
5. 6
6. 8
7. square, rectangle

Page 55
1. 3, 2, 6
2. 4, 3, 12
3. 5, 4, 20
4. 7, 5, 35

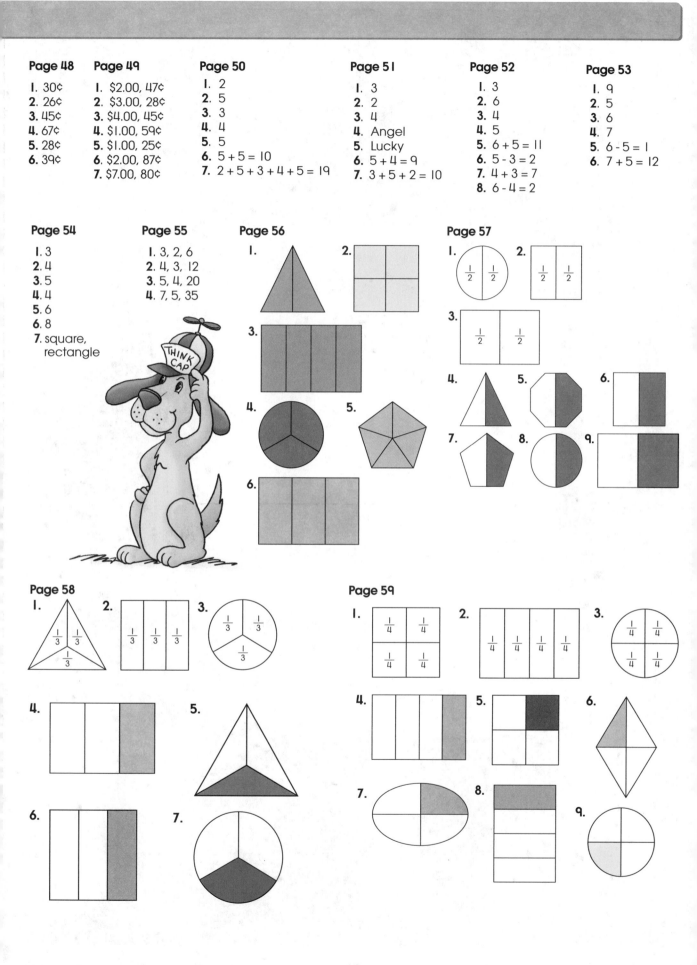

Page 56

Page 57

Page 58

Page 59

Award
Great Job!

_____
Name

finished **Math Basics 2**
from
School Zone Publishing.

Math Basics 2 **02202**